RAISING

BADASS HUMANS

14 Intentional Connections that Nurture Your Child's Emotional Intelligence and Sense of Self-Worth

---

Special <u>FREE</u> Bonus Gift for You
To become more self-aware and align with your truth go to <u>www.freegiftfromkat.com</u>
for your FREE BONUS RESOURCES

BY KAT MULLIN, HHP

Aligning Purpose Publishing
Seattle, Washington

D1715588

Published by
Aligning Purpose Publishing
Seattle, Washington

ISBN: 9798363253966
Photo Credits:
valwestoverphotography.com:page 7, back and spine cover photo
Keris Binder: page 8, 130,
Cover Image: Kpargeter at Freepik.com:
Cover Design: StarrLoutsis@aligningpurpose.com
Printed in the United States of America
December 2022

What Others Are Saying About Kat and Her Strategies

"Kat's radiant energy is infectious! I feel so lucky to have been able to connect with such a genuine soul! I rarely follow anyone on social media, but I will always log on to soak in the realism of Kat and her evolving growth. Her views are massively refreshing and relatable!"

~ Jama Young, Mom of Two

"What Kat talks about moves me to tears. Her impact is huge, and it will be getting only more powerful. Her methods may turn out to be a great gift for you and your kids."

~ Valeriya Ordinartseva, Happiness Coach and Founder of Made in Childhood

"Kat has a gift! I am so friggin glad she chooses to use and share her knowledge."

~ Carina Ritchie, Mom of Two

"Kat has so much experience and knowledge! It is her duty to share her passion. I admire her confidence and vulnerability"

~ Kris Spivey, LMT, HHP, CPT

"Kat helped me at a time I was working a job that left me feeling unworthy at times. She gave me a fresh perspective and showed me how to deal with things in a loving and caring way while ultimately taking care of myself first. She reminded me I am amazing, and I can do this! I thank Kat from the bottom of my heart for helping me move in a new direction in my life."

~ Sabrina O., Entrepreneurial Mom

"Kat's coaching and natural intuitive abilities are amazing. As somebody who recently got married, Kat helped me feel complete within myself. We worked through the things I didn't want which allowed me to see the things that I do want. Kat is able to get through to the root of the problem and help get past it faster. She can help you do whatever you want in your life too."

~ Sara N., Stress Xpert

"During my Breakthrough Session with Kat she helped me become aware of the root cause of my lack of motivation and eliminate it. The most beautiful thing is the positive impact it has had on my family. Thank you Kat!"

~ Carol Ivette, Mindset & Performance Coach and Serial Entrepreneur

"I had the honor of working with Kat as my Neuro-Linguistic Practitioner. She had a very quick and effective method that she installed in me so that I could have joy, confidence, and motivation in an instant. It was truly effective and is so wonderful to be able to initiate these feelings at the drop of a hat. She is a very kind and gentle person. Her energy was wonderful. I loved working with her."

~ Anneline Duffield, Master NLP Breakthrough Coach

"When I came to Kat, I was feeling stuck in my career. I felt unsure and confused. We worked on communicating more effectively. She also helped me to find out my true core values. This allowed me to revamp my business model. I now feel more aligned within myself and with what my business is projecting. Thank you so much Kat!"

~Julie Sanders Schlatter, Empowerment Coach and Co-Founder Meta Mind Masters

"During our coaching session Kat helped me feel comfortable and relaxed. I was resolving things that were getting in my way of being truly authentic with myself. I now feel like I am more comfortable in my skin, and ready to do what I love without worrying about anyone else's thoughts or opinions."

~ Meisha Marshall, Mother of One and Marriage Coach

Motivate and Inspire Others!

"Share This Book"

Retail $14.95

Special Quantity Discounts

5-20 Books	$12.95
21-99 Books	$10.95
100-499 Books	$9.95
500-999 Books	$8.95
1,000+ Books	$7.95

To place an order contact:

www.katmullin.com

kat@katmullin.com

The Ideal Professional Speaker For Your Next Event!

Any organization that wants to develop their people to become "extraordinary," needs to hire Kat Mullin for a keynote and/or workshop training!

TO CONTACT OR BOOK Kat Mullin TO SPEAK:

website:
www.katmullin.com
Email:
 kat@katmullin.com

The Ideal Coach For You!

If you're ready to overcome challenges, have major breakthroughs and align with your purpose, then you will love having Kat Mullin as your coach!

TO CONTACT Kat Mullin

website:
www.katmullin.com
Email:
kat@katmullin.com

Dedication

It is with incredible love that I dedicate this book to my four Badass Humans! They are my greatest teachers in life and have helped me grow and heal in tremendous ways.

To our Forever Baby, Taylor Hope: You showed me my purpose in life, and I am forever grateful to you. Until we meet again in the Spiritual World, Daddy and I hold you in our hearts always.

To Samantha, Sydney, and Sawyer: I could never express my love for you amazing souls enough! You show me every day what I need to work on to be a better mother and person. You love me unconditionally even when I am not at my best. Each one of you has made my life so much better in different ways. Thank you for the love, the laughs, and yes even for the tears. I love you all forever and ever!

Table Of Contents

What is a BADASS HUMAN?

/'bad,as (h)yoo-muhn/

A person who stands in their truth without fear of judgement.

Brave **A**uthentic **D**ecisive **A**ccepting **S**trong **S**upportive

Honest **U**nstoppable **M**indful **A**ccountable **N**onjudgmental

A Badass Human is a person who lives their truth. Not society's truth. Not their family's truth. Not their friend's truth. Not an organization's truth. THEIR TRUTH!

Living one's truth is not an easy thing to do in this world! It takes a lot of Self-Love, Confidence, Bravery, and Self-Respect to choose your own path in life.

Badass Humans are the cycle breakers. The ones who follow their hearts. Not what makes them popular. They live the life that makes them happy and fulfilled. And they encourage others to do the same.

1

My Message to YOU!

"Mom, could you please not yell at me today in front of my friends? I haven't told them how much you yell at me."

We had been getting ready to go on Samantha's first-grade class field trip to the zoo. I was so excited to finally be a parent volunteer. With two younger children at home, it was rare I could get away. Her innocent question stopped me in my tracks. I felt like I had been hit by a train. My sweet little six-year-old was ashamed of how she was treated in her own home.

You would suppose the words spoken by my curly-haired, blue-eyed girl would catapult me to make a lasting change. Sadly, they did not.

How did it come to this? Why wasn't I the Mom I thought I would be? While I was pregnant, I had visions of my little one and I doing yoga and meditating together every morning. Instead, too many of our days were filled with yelling and tears to get out the door in time, do our nightly routine, or hell, simply to exist. Too many times I watched my young babies shrink away from me, cover their ears, and cry because I lost control and was screaming again.

You would suppose the words spoken by my curly haired blue-eyed girl would catapult me to make a lasting change. Sadly, they did not. Not for lack of trying, mind you. I told myself I would stop yelling. Most nights, I would lie in bed convincing myself that tomorrow would be different. Tomorrow I would remain calm. Tomorrow I wouldn't scream so hard I almost pass out. I was sure of it!

Of course, there were the peaceful days too. I have countless memories in which we laughed and smiled and truly enjoyed being together. My social media posts surely conveyed a happy and loving family! In my mind though, the happy times were moments sprinkled in between the hard times. Was that true? Sometimes yes. Mostly no. Yet raising my voice at little kids on an almost daily basis was not acceptable. Something had to be done!

I read many parenting books and took online classes that promised me a peaceful home free of chaos. And they worked! For a little bit anyway. And then, within a couple of weeks, my old patterns would creep back in. I would get triggered again, and the yelling would start again. Then the guilt and shame would come rushing back like a tidal wave. Especially since I should have known better. I mean, I read the books and took the classes!

I started to get furious with the Universe. I used to ask, "Why would you give me these little souls? I don't deserve them. They need better than ME!" I loved my kids deeply, but I felt like I was screwing them up. This broke my heart. I found myself sobbing on the floor in a fetal position more than once.

In each of my kids' baby books there is a page to write them a letter. Without fail I wrote to each of my babies that my biggest wish for them is that they grow up comfortable in their own skin. I mistakenly thought I could raise them to be confidently themselves even though I wasn't.

I don't remember the first time I heard the term "Generational Patterns", but when I did things started to make sense for me. They can also be referred to as Generational Cycles, Legacies, or Curses. Generational Patterns are learned behaviors, habits, beliefs, reactions, perspectives and so on that are passed down through our family lineage. Most of us are unaware that we are running our lives based on this programming we inherited.

Not all the patterns are bad of course. I can look at another person's perspective unbiasedly thanks to my father. He loved to play devil's advocate with me when I was upset with a situation. I am grateful to my mother for teaching me the importance of proper manners and that laughing is an essential part of life.

Unfortunately, many of the patterns we have been handed down are unhealthy. I come from a long line of screamers on my mother's side. No matter how many times I swore I would never yell at my kids when I became a mother, here I was screaming my head off. From both sides of my family, I learned that we don't talk about our issues. We sweep them under the rug and ignore them! If I was unhappy with someone, I had no clue how to express it to them because I was taught confrontation was taboo. At the same time, I was taught to kick someone's ass if they "disrespected" me or one of my own. It was very confusing to grow up with these conflicting beliefs. As an adult I can now separate them and see I was inadvertently taught that drama and fighting triumphed over healthy conversations.

Becoming aware of the patterns instilled in me was only the beginning of the healing process. The more conscious I became of where my reactions stemmed from, the more guilt and shame I had for still not being able to control them.

I started to recognize when something one of my kids said triggered me to feel like I wasn't good enough. Recognizing it didn't stop me from getting pissed off and yelling at them though. When no one would jump up and do what I requested it activated a deep seeded conviction I had that no one listens to me. This confirmed a limiting belief of mine that I didn't matter. My screaming and yelling had everything to do with my unresolved traumas and nothing to do with my children's perceived bad behavior. Yet I had no clue how to stop reacting to it. I made excuses that I didn't have the time or money to get help with breaking the patterns I was becoming so mindful of.

A few more years passed. They were full of ups, downs, and lots of big life changes. I would feel like things were finally coming together just to fall back further. My husband, Matthew, was simultaneously struggling with his own unhealthy patterns. What looked like an amazing life on the outside, and was in many ways, was full of chaos and reactivity behind closed doors.

My worst fear for my kids started to come true. They started to become us. I could see the patterns of anger, depression, low self-esteem, and people pleasing rearing their ugly heads. This is what finally pushed me over the edge. This was NOT okay!!! I was aware of what was happening, and it was my responsibility to make changes. No more excuses!

Diving headfirst into my "healing journey", I started meditating every morning, read some amazing books on personal development, and took self-love courses. The most important thing I did though, was hire different life coaches to help me gain clarity on how I wanted to show up as a mom, for myself, in my relationships, and in my career. It was the coaches that helped me make the lasting changes. I realized I had to start with my own growth so I could become what my kids needed.

At the same time, I knew my kids couldn't wait for me to be "healed" before I could be there for them too. I needed to be present for them in the moment. I discovered the best ways to connect with my family and start breaking the generational patterns that no longer served us. A different way of parenting became very clear to me. And in the process, I discovered my new purpose in life.

To set future generations free by inspiring parents to slow down and be present now. Allowing both the parents and their children to break the unhealthy patterns that hold them back so they can live their lives full of authenticity, confidence, joy and passion.

This purpose arose from seeing what my kids needed in order to be comfortable in their own skin. They needed connection more than anything. For me to be fully present with them and accept them as they are. The bonus benefit was how much this quality time helped me to accept myself as well.

What this means for YOU...

You do not have to wait to be "healed" before you can show up for your kids. I use quotations around healed, healing, and healing journey because you are never fully healed. There are always going to be layers to reveal, triggers that get activated, patterns to be recognized, and inner work to be done. Healing is a lifelong journey. Perhaps a better way to describe this process is a Journey of Self-Awareness. As you start your own personal journey it will have a ripple effect on everyone around you. Letting your child be a part of the process as you realign with your truth will help them connect them to theirs, and the benefits they will reap from you choosing to be present with them today are immeasurable.

Raising Badass Humans is born from my own experience of trial and error. Meaning you will not have to try all the different ways I did in order to succeed on your own "healing" path with your family. I share with you the connections I started making with my kids that took me from feeling like I was a failure as a parent to confidently knowing I am the best mother for my kiddos. These are the intentional ways you can build a relationship with each of your children that is grounded in trust and unconditional love. These are the ways you can help your child grow into who they are meant to be.

Am I a perfect parent now? Hell no! For one, I cuss regularly, and some frown upon that. I am who I am! Seriously though, I still get triggered. My old patterns still grab a hold of me, and I have times my ego takes over and my voice raises. In other words, I still lose my shit! However, I lose it less often and I have tools now to recognize when I'm being reactive so I can calm down faster and choose to respond differently. So, yes, I still have days I am not 100% proud of my parenting. What I know is this... When I do reset and use the methods I share in this book, my whole family is better off because of it!

When should you start implementing these techniques? The sooner the better! And it's never too late. In a perfect world everyone would learn all of this before they have children. Starting on your path of self-awareness while also raising little ones is definitely more challenging. It is absolutely doable though. Keep in mind children have an imprinting period of 0-7 years. After the age of 7 it becomes increasingly more difficult to change the patterns that have already been instilled in them. If your children are in this age group, I urge you to start NOW! Again, it is still possible if they are over 7 years of age, so don't think you shouldn't bother. My oldest was just turning 9 when I started this process. Honestly, I am a firm believer in "better late than never". I don't care if your child is 60 years old. You can still make a difference in their life when you choose to be present for them.

What is a Present Parent?

Playful **R**espectful **E**ncouraging **S**afe-place **E**ngaging **N**urturing **T**rusting

Patient **A**ffectionate **R**eliable **E**mpathetic **N**imble **T**houghtful

Give your children the gift of a Healthier You...
DO IT FOR THEM!

*Side note: I use the term "parent/s" throughout this book to keep it simple. I am really referring to anyone who is important in a child's life. This book is also for Parents to Be, Grandparents, Aunts, Uncles, Foster Parents, Stepparents, Teachers, Coaches, et

Section One

QUALITY TIME

If you want to change the world,

Go home and love your family.

~Mother Theresa~

Why Quality Time?

The single most important thing you can give your child is your time. Nothing will build their confidence, give them high self-esteem, create a trusting bond between you both, and assure their trust in who they are like knowing they matter. And you are who they want to matter to most!

Kids have basic needs beyond food, clothing, and shelter. Attention is one of those necessities. Like everyone else in the world children long to be heard, seen, and loved. Everyone needs to know they are important. When a child does not receive an adequate amount of positive attention, they may begin to act out to get you to notice them and fill their attention cup. To a child's mind, negative attention is better than no attention. The best prevention for "bad" behavior is to give them positive attention before they are in need of attention.

Sadly, in previous years society's message to parents was that kids didn't matter. They were to be seen and not heard. Their opinions had no bearing. They didn't have emotional needs. They were expected to be in control of their feelings and not express them negatively even when the adults around them could not manage that difficult task. If they could not, they were punished for it.

Sound a little dramatic? Maybe. But this way of childrearing was not uncommon over the past couple of generations at least. And a lot of us adults are now paying the price for it. Many of us have

> You can choose to raise your children differently.

depression, anger management issues, low confidence, feelings of low self-worth, are people pleasers and so on. You don't have to continue this cycle with your children. You can choose to raise your children differently. Go against the grain of society and do what's best for your unique family.

Connection #1

Truly Listen to Your Child

One of the best ways you can show up for your child is to truly listen when they talk to you. In this busy society where distractions are so easily available, people have lost sight of what it means to give someone their full attention. Your focus is divided between work, home life, social media, television, the bills that are due, what you need at the grocery store, etc.

According to an article on PeacefulParent.com*, "Quality time deepens our empathy for our child". It is vital your child knows you hear them. That what they have to say means something to you. Many of the things they want to tell you about may seem trivial. Remember it is not to them. To them it's their whole world in the moment. Maybe you've heard all about their favorite cartoon character, the book they're reading, or the same joke a hundred times on repeat. Maybe you think your head will explode if you must hear about the toy they want and all the cool things it can do one more time. Listen anyway! Listen to these "little" things now because one day what they need to tell you will be very important and if they didn't feel heard when they were younger, they won't trust they can come to you when they are older. When problems consist of being teased, peer pressure, alcohol and drugs, romantic relationships, and/or sex, you will want them to know you can be trusted with it all.

My most recent example happened as I was writing this section of the book. Samantha called me from her Gizmo watch to come pick her and her sister, Sydney, up at the park. The park is inside our neighborhood and only takes a couple of minutes to walk to. I wanted to say, "No, I'm busy and you two are capable of walking." I could hear in her voice she was upset though so I closed my computer and went to get them. Turns out the other kids at the playground started playing Spin the Bottle, and it made my girls very uncomfortable. We talked about it for a bit, and I made sure they knew how proud I was of them for calling me and leaving when something didn't feel right to them. Then they went inside to play together. I sat outside reflecting on how when I was 12, I was desperate to belong and fit in. I did play Spin the Bottle and Truth or Dare, and I never told my parents about it!

How do you get to that point? The point where your kids are comfortable calling you to get them out of a bad situation. How do you build that trust? The key is to actively listen to them now. Do not just listen with your ears. Listen with every part of you because they know when you are only half paying attention. They know when they aren't fully being heard. And it doesn't feel good to them. When they talk to you put down all distractions and look them in the eyes (unless you're driving). Put the phone down, mute the tv, turn your body to face them, and get down to their level so you're not towering over them. Shut off the inner dialogue of what else you want or should be doing in that moment. Stop planning your response before you have heard them out. Just listen!

Is it always possible to stop what you are doing when your child starts to speak? Of course not. There is a way to teach them patience when that is the case. Have a talk with your children about how to politely get your attention if you are in the middle of something when they want to speak with you. Come up with a system that works for all of you. For us it is gently putting a hand on my shoulder and wait for me to respond. The hand must be still on me because poking me repeatedly will automatically trigger my nervous system to snap! Don't expect them to be perfect with your new system right away. It takes time for it to

16

become their new norm. If they forget, gently remind them.

When your child does implement your new calm way of getting your attention, you have two choices. You can immediately stop what you are doing and give them your full attention, or you can tell them you are in the middle of something important and will be with them shortly. With practice your children will develop more patience. They will understand waiting is worth it to get all of you instead of a distracted version of you. When you are deciding the best way for them to let you know they need to talk to you, explain to them that what they have to say is so incredibly important to you and you don't want to miss any of it. Sometimes what you are already doing is also important and needs your focus in the moment. If they could just give you a couple of minutes to finish, they will be rewarded by being the center of your attention. Don't leave them waiting too long though! Their attention span is short lived. My son, Sawyer, will call me out and say something like, "Mom, put down your phone and look me in the eyes so I know you can hear me!".

It is crucial to remember your child does not only communicate with their words. In fact, words are only 7% of communication. Tone of voice and body language make up the other 93%. Pay very close attention to both of those. When Samantha called me to pick her and Sydney up from the park it was more the tone of her voice than the words she was using that let me know she really needed me. If your child tells you they are fine, but their shoulders are slumped or their fists are clenched, they are not fine. Maybe they don't have the words to express what is bothering them yet. Maybe they don't know what is bothering them. Remind them you are here for them when they are ready to talk. Just saying that little sentence instills so much faith in them that they are not in it alone.

Take notice of changes in their behavior as well. If there is a significant change in the way they act, there may be something going on under the surface. A lot of times children believe they are fine when they are not. Pay attention to the little things. Are they more reactive than usual, not sleeping well, extra needy, suddenly scared of something, or doing anything out of the norm? For example, some kids may start wetting the bed after a big life change. A big move to a new place, for instance. They may seem fine emotionally and mentally but something else is giving you the clue they need you. I've heard of some kids who pull their eyebrow hairs or eyelashes out when something is unconsciously bothering them. "Listen" to these things! They are communicating something important to you. Ask them if something is wrong. If they say no, remind them that you are present and ready to talk when they are. You can gently guide them by acknowledging that sometimes big changes can be scary and may make some people nervous. That may be enough for them to realize what's going on and be able to talk about it. Basically, let them know they are seen and heard. It makes all the difference.

While words are only 7% of communication, they have so much power! Words have different meanings for each individual and that can lead to misunderstandings. Which is why I created a downloadable E-book for you. **The 8 Keys to Effective Communication** helps strengthen your relationships with all your loved ones by greatly decreasing miscommunication.

Go to www.katmullin.com to download your free copy.

Connection #2

Intentional Family Time

I tell my coaching clients that "Being in the same space does NOT equal quality time together." In an article on VeryWellFamily.com* the author says, "Quality time may be more important than the quantity of time". I would argue it IS more important! Work, school, activities, and chores are time consuming. Too many families are just going through the motions right now. When they are home at the same time, they are tired and want to relax. Sitting in the same room as each other doing mindless activities like watching tv or staring at their computers and phones does not create a connection and does not count as quality time together. I am not saying it is never okay to "veg out". However, it is vital that you and your family set aside specific times to be intentionally present with each other.

Get back to the basics. Sit and have a meal together! Not many families can do this nightly anymore with their overactive schedules. Do it when you can and do not allow phones at the table. I see so many parents complaining their kids are always on their phones. It is up to you to set the boundaries with electronics. No phones or tv during dinner time is a good place to begin setting those limits. Use this time to catch up with each other.

Family meetings once a month are a great way to start building bonds. Your kid may hem and haw about them at first because it seems boring to sit and talk. They may feel differently when they become aware of the connection that happens. This is an opportunity to catch up on where everyone is at with their thoughts and emotions. How do they feel about school, hobbies, activities, friendships, and/or home life? It is a time to share wins and losses. For everyone to get a chance to suggest new ways of doing things. Talk about what is working and what is not. If a change does need to be made in the way the household is run, have one person write down everyone's suggestions without judgment. After all ideas are written down, go through them one by one to agree on what to implement. We like to have the person talking hold a "baton", so everyone knows whose turn it is to speak and not interrupt them. Honestly, we use whatever we have handy. A remote or a stuffed animal do the trick!

Weekly game nights are a fun way to bring the family together. Find a night of the week that everyone is home to participate. You can take turns letting family members choose the game you play. Some of our favorites are Uno, Sorry, and Life. No distractions should be allowed. Everyone who has a phone should turn it to silent and put it down. Televisions should be off as to not draw anyone's focus away from the games. Movie night can replace game night periodically but not frequently. Connections are not easily made while everyone focuses on the screen. It does, however, allow for family discussions about the movie afterwards. If you do choose a movie for family night, I highly suggest a comedy. Laughing together is an amazing way to bond!

Get outside as a family together too! Nature and fresh air are essential to not only physical but mental health as well. My family's favorite outdoor activity is hiking. We call ourselves *The Badass Hiking Family*. For us it's one of the best ways to connect. I started taking my kids hiking regularly when they were 7, 4, and 1.5 years old. They didn't get the point right away. I heard a lot of "We are just walking Mom! This is boring! Why are we doing this?" It didn't take them long to see the benefits. I found giving them a goal to reach, like a waterfall to see or awesome rocks to scramble on, really motivated them. Wasn't long until they were cheering me on to finish if I thought we should turn around! Find what outside activity you and your family enjoy doing together. Bike rides, kayaking, swimming, walking, or whatever gets you out in the sun enjoying the day as a family.

I know it's not easy to fit all of these activities into your family's busy lives. If you can't set an exact schedule for these intentional times together, do make them happen as often as possible. You can always make time for what is important to you. Actively look for ways your family can connect more to build trust and lasting bonds. You will be so happy with the benefits you all receive!

Connection #3

Date Your Kids

THIS! This is the #1 thing I recommend
to every parent I coach!

Each parenting course I took recommended, first and foremost, to spend uninterrupted time with your children. They suggested to spend 10 minutes a day playing with your child with no distractions at all. This seemed simple enough. Who can't free up 10 minutes of their day every day? Well depending on how many kids you have it starts to add up. I needed to find 30 minutes a day for my kiddos. Still doesn't sound hard but it was! Add to the mix that I had to have something for the other two kids to do while playing with one of them. I tried bringing one outside and the other two would follow. They would watch me play with the one and continue to interrupt to ask when it was their turn? They were young, and it was not easy for them to have patience. I could have let them zone out in front of the tv but then the one I was playing with felt like they were missing out since I didn't allow a ton of screen time. It just didn't work for us. I tried giving them each longer time once per week. We ran into the same issues. If we were in the presence of the other two, they were the distraction!

That's when I decided it would be best if we got away from the house. We implemented monthly dates in which myself and one child would leave the house for a few hours. THIS WAS THE MAGIC! Somehow the other two would not be jealous because they knew their turn was coming to have me all to themselves too. And they got to stay home and have special time playing with just each other. Two usually play together better than three!

The key to these dates is to let it be all about the child you are with that day. Let them choose what you do. Within reason of course. You can't be heading to an amusement park every time! The point of letting them pick the activity is for them to know what they enjoy doing matters to you. It says to them, "You are important to me." So, if it's something you can reasonably do, say YES!

As you continue to spend this one-on-one time with your child you will become aware of all the benefits it has. This is when the trust between you two grows. These dates prove to your child that you are there for them. You choose to spend your precious time with them and that is huge! With each excursion they will start to open up to you more and more. This is when you will hear about who their friends are, what issues they are facing socially and academically, what they are interested in, and how they feel about important issues. This is a time to truly listen. Don't try to fix or solve their problems. If you have valuable advice, ask them first if they want it. This way they know they are heard. They'll know what they feel and think matters. These dates foster the growth of their confidence and self-esteem. Truly nothing will build these for your child like your undivided attention and time. Prioritize dates!

By the way, the benefits are not only for your child's growth and for your relationship together. There are many benefits for you as well. Letting your inner child out to play during these dates increases your happiness levels, allows more laughter into your life, and gets you physical exercise. All great for your mental and physical health!

The earlier you can start "dating" your child the better. However, it is never too late to start. Your teenager may not be interested in this time together at first. Their own social life is their priority. Don't give up on them though. After a few dates they are likely going to start trusting you. They will see you have no agenda other than being there for them. You may not want to call them "dates" though. Samantha started feeling uncomfortable with that terminology around the age of ten. So, we say things like, "our time together, mother-daughter time, one-on-one time" instead.

One concern I notice parents sometimes have is the added expense of the dates. I am here to tell you this doesn't have to cost anything. Kids love free dates as much as they love the ones in which you splurge financially. For them it is all about being with YOU! The memories you make are priceless, and experiences will always matter more to your child than any material object. If times are tight, give them free options to pick from. It is still important they choose the activity even if you give the ideas.

My kids and I created a PDF of FREE Date Ideas for you and your kiddos! Go to www.katmullin.com to download your free copy.

I would love to hear from you! Contact me to let me know what your favorite dates, free or not, are to do with your children. We could always use fresh ideas!

Connection #4
Take Advantage of the Little Moments

I n between dates be sure to take advantage of any moments you can be present with your child. You will find there are lots of opportunities to stop and just be with them. You can allow the dishes to go unwashed just a little longer or the laundry to sit unfolded. These things were beyond hard for me to do at first as I used to be a clean freak. Everything had to have its place and dishes couldn't sit in my sink after a meal was finished. I am glad I've let go of those tendencies. You will never regret letting the housework go in exchange for a bonding moment with your little human.

Look for the moments. Some days two of my kids go out to play while one chooses to stay behind. I may first be wishing they would go play with friends too so I can have some time to work or get the house in order. Then they ask me to play a board game or something together. After my initial resistance, I realize it is a chance to connect with them and I am grateful.

On family hikes one of the kids may start lagging, so I stay back with them. Next thing I know we are in some deep conversation about an issue I didn't even know they were having. I feel honored they trust me enough to let me into their world. Again, I'm grateful for the opportunity to connect one-on-one. Even in the middle of a family day.

Reading at bedtime is always a great time to be present with each other. They snuggle right up to me as I read the pages to them. We laugh at the photos together. We also use this time for them to sharpen their own skills and read to me. When we put the book down there may be more snuggle time. Sawyer still wants me to sing him to sleep. I am tone def and have a horrible singing voice, so I know this is one more way he chooses to be present with me. Bedtime snuggles are when I get the most adoration and hear things like, "You're the best Mom ever!" or "Thank you for being someone I can talk to." There's nothing better than words of affirmation from my littles!

At first, I got caught up in having to always be *fully* present in order to play with one of my kids. So, I would say no if I was doing the dishes, laundry, or any other chore. I've come to realize that it is okay to play while doing all the things too.

Sawyer asks me to play Superheroes a lot. He is fine with me pretending to be Wonder Woman or Bionic Woman as I clean if I talk with him while I do it. These moments are important too, but they should not replace the times you are fully present. Consider these times an added bonus.

Section Two

EMBRACE EMOTIONS

It is our job as parents to TEACH our kids

how to feel their emotions.

Not to PUNISH them for "bad" behavior

because they don't instinctually know how.

~Kat Mullin~

How Your Child's Brain Works

In my opinion, holding space for your child's big emotions is the hardest job a parent has. And the most important. They don't know how to regulate these overwhelming sensations and that stresses them out. When they are stressed, the tantrums start! Personally, my biggest trigger is my kids' giant emotions. When they start reacting to them my nervous system lights up like the Fourth of July and I want it to stop immediately. I wish I could say I always handle these times with grace. I cannot say that! I've had my own tantrums in response to theirs more than I care to admit. Understanding how the brain works has helped me immensely with being able to respond calmly to the meltdowns.

I am not a scientist nor a doctor of any kind. I am a parent who researches the best ways to support my child's emotional development and well-being. The book I have found most helpful in understanding how the brain develops is *The*

Whole-Brain Child*. This book goes into the science behind brain development and how it relates to your child and his/her emotions. Having an understanding of this information is extremely important for you as a parent. I will do my best to explain the basics in simple terms. I recommend you do more research on this topic on your own.

The brain not only has the left and right hemispheres, it also has lower and upper sections as well. Let's start with left and right. The right side of the brain develops first and is all about the way something makes you feel. It interprets non-verbal cues like body language and tone of voice, and cares more about the big picture instead of the details. The right brain is intuitive, emotional and thinks in terms of personal memories. Infants and toddlers live in the right brain which allows them to always be in the moment. They don't care about schedules and being on time. They will stop everything to literally smell a flower and admire it. Being in their right brain is also why their emotions run high. Everything seems so dramatic to them because it really is. An epic meltdown doesn't seem unreasonable to the child who just discovered you're out of their favorite yogurt flavor. They haven't tapped into their logical brain yet to comprehend you can buy more later. Can you see now why telling a toddler to stop crying and be reasonable won't work?

An important fact to know is that the left side of the brain doesn't develop until approximately 7 years of age. This side is all about logic. It craves order, routines, lists, and is very literal. For instance, you tell one of your kids to not hit the other and their response is, "I didn't hit her, I kicked her!" They don't quite understand figures of speech either. One of my favorite examples of this was when my niece told her young daughter to "hold her horses" as she ran outside for something quickly. When my niece came back in the house her daughter was standing there holding all her horse figurines!

Now on to the lower and upper brain sections. The lower brain is all about survival. It controls your basic functions like breathing and reactions. Do you jump if a spider comes down in front of your face? You can thank your lower brain for that reflex. It is where you find the brain stem and limbic region which is responsible for flight, freeze, or fight responses. Your child lives here! There is no logic happening in the lower brain.

The upper brain is the rational section of your brain. It is where you find the cerebral cortex, specifically the prefrontal cortex which has to do with decision making, social behavior like empathy and morality, personality traits, self-awareness, and control over one's emotions. Here's the kicker, the upper brain does not fully develop until your mid-twenties! **Read that again**. The upper brain does not fully develop until your mid-twenties!!

> The upper brain does not fully develop until your mid-twenties!

Therefore, your young child can't grasp the concept when you are trying to negotiate with them. They aren't trying to manipulate you or be disrespectful. It doesn't matter to them that you do your best to be fair. If they feel you are being mean when you turn off the tv, they are going to express that to you! And no amount of talking to them about how you gave them a 15-minute warning is going to make a difference.

This doesn't mean your kid will be completely unreasonable until they are grown adults. Everyone matures at different rates, and the good news is, you can help your child's advancement in this area by being conscious of where they are with their brain development. You can guide them to integrate their right and left brains as well as their lower and upper brains by how you treat them when they are "in crisis".

Another extremely crucial fact to understand is that when a person's emotions are elevated, child or adult, they are in their lower brain and CANNOT access their upper logical brain in the moment. The prefrontal cortex literally shuts down and cannot be reached. Trying to reason with anyone who is emotionally charged will only lead to more frustration. So, telling your child to "knock it off, stop crying, just do what I told you to" will never work. They cannot stop. They cannot hear you! The best thing you can do is not take it personally and wait until they are calm to talk with them. It is better for them if you can stay in their presence in a calm state and just be there for them. Easier said than done, I know! If their meltdown is triggering you and you can't remain calm during it, go in another room until it passes.

*Side note: If your child's tantrums are to the point they are putting themselves or others in danger you may want to consider seeking the help of a medical professional. I am referring to the normal everyday meltdowns that drive us crazy!

Connection #5

Validate Your Child's Feelings

"Mommy, I feel sad, and I don't know why."

Kids do not always understand why they feel the way they do. It is vitally important that you do not deny or dismiss their feelings. They are probably already confused and if you deny they are feeling the way they say they are, you will undermine their trust in themselves. They will not feel safe expressing feelings and will start to believe they are wrong about what they are experiencing. This will lead to a buildup of unexpressed emotions which later come out in unhealthy ways. Repressed emotions can show up in unwanted behavior and/or in physical ailments like headaches or stomachaches.

Parents don't even realize they are denying their child's feelings. I see this all the time. A child falls and scrapes their knee and are told "Don't cry. You are okay. Be a big girl/boy. It doesn't hurt that bad." I know this is the parent's way of trying to calm the kid and make everything better, but it does the complete opposite. Your child does not feel ok and needs to be able to say so! They are still a big boy/girl even if they cry. It does hurt! Try saying things like, "I see you are hurt. Can I get you an icepack? It's okay to cry. Would you like a hug or a kiss? How can I help you?"

My Samantha needs a moment to herself when she first gets hurt. It used to be a struggle between us until I figured that out. I would automatically go into help mode, and she would get upset with me. I would then get angry at her for being upset with me when I just wanted to help. Next, I tried ignoring it when she got hurt, and she would think I didn't care. I felt like I couldn't win. It was not a fun cycle for either of us. Until I learned to simply say, "I am here when you are ready to tell me how I can help you.".

Have you ever felt sad, anxious, or angry and had no clue why? This happens to your little one too. You may want to soothe them by saying things like, "There's nothing to be sad about. Cheer up!". If you tell them there's no reason to feel the way they do, they will think something is wrong with them which will cause anxiety inside of them. Tell them it's okay to feel sad (or however they feel). Tell them they don't have to know why they feel the way they do. That there usually is a reason for it even if we can't see what that reason is in that moment, and it's important to allow themselves to feel it. Simply be present with them while they work through it. Sometimes they just need a hug or for you to sit silently with them. Sometimes they will want to talk about it. They may even discover what was bothering them as they talk with you, but it's okay if they don't.

Then there are the times the reason for their feelings is obvious. Yet they may not know what the emotion is they are feeling. You can help them name the feeling so they can get to the other side of it faster. For example, when your child cries because their ice cream fell to the ground, don't tell them it is no big deal. To them it is! If you say, "You can just get a new ice cream", they will say "But I wanted that one!!!". Instead use this opportunity to help them integrate their right and left brain. Connect with them first on an emotional level by helping them label how they feel. "I see you're sad about your ice cream falling. I would be sad if my ice cream fell too." Give them time to work through the sadness before trying to bring logic to the table. Once they are calm you can offer them that new ice cream.

This goes for all emotions. Are they frustrated because they are struggling with their math homework? Are they angry their brother got one more candy than they did? Are they scared to sleep without a nightlight? Whatever the emotion, meet them where they are first. Help them label the feeling and talk about it so they can truly feel it. They can't move past an emotion without feeling it first. It is helpful to have an emotion wheel chart handy.

Validating their feelings is an absolute must for your child to develop emotional intelligence. Allowing them to feel and express what is going on for them shows you accept them as they are. It builds their trust in both themselves and in you. This is a huge confidence builder!

> Validating their feelings is an absolute must for your child to develop emotional intelligence.

Connection #6

Go Through the Negative

When one of my children would focus on something that upset them, I would tell them to find something positive to focus on instead. Then I would get frustrated when it didn't work! Here's a perfect example...

For Samantha's 6th birthday party, she was very clear she wanted to invite only a handful of friends. We were having it at a park, and I couldn't understand why she wouldn't invite all her friends and classmates. Instead of listening to her desires or asking her why she wanted only a few people there, I invited everyone under the sun! At least it felt that way to her. I let my ego get in the way because I didn't want to appear rude by leaving anyone out.

As the guests began to arrive, she got more and more upset. "MOM! You invited them too!!!" One of my friends told me that she thanked Samantha for inviting her and her kids to the party. Samantha's response was, "I didn't. My mom did.".

When it was time for cake, we gathered around the picnic table at the park. Because the park is a public place, we were not the only people enjoying the facilities. A little girl around 3 years old saw the cake and got excited. She asked if she could have a piece too and I said yes. Now Samantha was even more upset because it was her party, and I didn't allow her to answer the little girl. I couldn't see what the big deal was. I was just being polite!

For the next 3.5 years this situation would come up periodically. Yes, you read that right. For 3.5 years this was an issue between the two of us. Samantha would say something like, "Remember my party when you let that girl I didn't even know have cake?" Or "Remember how you invited my whole class when I didn't want you to?" And every time my response was the same. I would immediately shut her down. Exhaustedly I would say things like, "Yes, I remember. Seriously, it was years ago. Can't you just let it go? I was trying to be nice! Why can't you think of one positive thing to say about that day?"

Then one day I got the best piece of advice from one of my life coaches. I was telling her about the situation and how I felt Samantha just couldn't let it go. She said to me, "Of course she can't. You never let her get through the negative. You must go through the negative with her before she can let go and focus on the positive." What??? How??? "Stop shutting her down and let her talk about it!"

> "You must go through the negative with her before she can let go and focus on the positive."

A couple of weeks later the party situation arose once again. This time I approached it differently. I said, "Let's talk about that." Samantha was surprised as she was used to me becoming agitated. I let her talk all about her feelings and why she was holding on to her frustration about it. She explained that she would have also given the girl cake but was upset I didn't let her make the decision since it was her party and her cake. However, what was really bothering her all this time was the fact I didn't listen to her about who to invite to the party and why. When she explained her reasoning for only wanting a handful of friends to come, I was blown away by her awareness. She had attended other kids' birthday parties where the whole class was there, and she noticed that the birthday kid's attention was spread too thin. They didn't have time to give each of their guests individual attention. Samantha remembered how excited she was to celebrate the birthday girl/boy, and she remembered how she felt when she didn't get to spend any time with them at their party. It was important to her that she be able to give each of her guests some one-on-one time, so they knew how much it meant to her that they came to her party. She knew if there were too many kids in attendance, she would not be able to give them each that special time with her.

I could not believe what I was hearing. How could I have not asked her right away why only inviting a few people was so important to her? Why didn't I listen from the beginning instead of letting my ego get in the way? I know Samantha. I know how kind and considerate she is. Yet somehow, I blocked that out of my mind when it suited my needs and I assumed she was just being impolite by not inviting everyone. When I finally stopped deflecting her feelings because they upset me and listened to her, I could clearly see the error of my ways. I immediately took responsibility for my actions and apologized for disrespecting her wishes for her 6th birthday party.

Can you guess what happened the next time this party came up in conversation? Samantha was able to talk about the things that were positive that

44

day. She thanked me for inviting one of her friends she hadn't put on her list because they were having a squabble in the moment. She said they were true friends, and she was happy to have her there after all. We talked about the fun she did have that day. She no longer holds on to any resentment towards me because I finally allowed her to feel the negative and get through it.

Fast forward to her 11th birthday party. She invited only who she wanted. Unfortunately, about half the kids were unable to make it. As we set up the decorations at the park, she expressed her disappointment that some of her friends couldn't be there. My instinct to be positive kicked in and suggested she be happy about who could attend. Her response was perfect. She said, "Mom, I'm choosing to feel this sadness right now. When my friends who can come start to arrive, I will choose to be happy with them." I love when they turn it around and remind me of the tools I do my best to equip them with!

One of the biggest mistakes parents can make is trying to cheer up a child who is upset before they are ready to be happy again. As you see, I have been guilty of this myself. No parent wants to see their child suffer. So, their natural instinct is to go into "fix-it mode". Maybe you try to distract them with laughter or remind them of what they could be grateful for, or just tell them to let it go. Whatever your method, it would be more beneficial to allow them to feel the negativity before redirecting them. Learning to stop protecting your child from their feelings and to help them go through the negative emotions will increase their emotional intelligence significantly.

In an article on JanetLansbury.com* she talks about how ACKNOWLEDGING your child's emotions is the key to their heart. I could not agree more! She makes several great points of how this is beneficial. I want to emphasize two of them here.

> ACKNOWLEDGING your child's emotions is the key to their heart.

1. "Acknowledging... fosters trust and encourages children to keep sharing their feelings."

2. "Acknowledging proves we are paying attention, makes a child feel understood, accepted, deeply loved, and supported."

Why did I share the story of Samantha's birthday party with you? What does it mean for you and your child? I share so you can see how important it is to allow your child to express when they are upset. Even when they are upset at you. I had to learn to not take it personally, listen with an open heart, accept her feelings, and take

46

responsibility for my part in it. When your child tells you that something you did hurt them, hear them without being defensive. See it as an opportunity for you to learn and grow because that's exactly what it is.

Thankfully not all their negative emotions will be about something you did. Be available to listen to them when they need to talk about any situation that is bothering them.

Connection #7

Be Their Best Role Model

Children don't become what you say,

they become who you are.

~Dean Graziosi~

Last year my son Sawyer needed extensive dental work. He was five at the time and previously had gold stars at all his dental appointments. I was shocked this time when I learned he went from no cavities to a mouthful. I brushed his teeth twice a day. How could this be? I was once a dental assistant and know a good deal about dental hygiene. My girls even floss every night. Yet, I slacked on the flossing with Sawyer. I had no good excuse for not flossing him nightly. Maybe it was because he is the third child, and I was getting lax. Maybe I just didn't have the energy to fight with him about it. I told myself it was because he had so much space between his teeth that he'd be fine. No matter the reason, when

I heard the news, the guilt hit me HARD! Especially on the day of his surgery. I watched as they put him under anesthesia, and let me tell you, it was not something I wish for any parent to witness. His eyes got wide, and he looked terrified right before he fell asleep. I stayed strong for his sake until the surgery was done.

Sawyer was groggy and confused when he first came out of the surgery. By the time we got home though, he was ready to play with his siblings and friends. He seemed perfectly over it. I was not! I was a mess of sadness and guilt. Logically I knew it was not my fault, but emotionally I needed time to get over feeling as if I failed him. My solution? I laid in bed most of the day and cried. My sweet Samantha came in and asked what she could do to cheer me up. I told her I appreciated her so much. That I was grateful she wanted to help me feel better, but that I needed to let myself feel the sadness so I could get through it. I reassured her I would be just fine after I grieved. And I was fine when I finally got out of bed. Most importantly, my kids got to witness how allowing myself to experience the emotions in the moment helped me to heal and move forward. And now I help Sawyer floss every night!

In the past I would have pushed these feelings down deep so I could carry on with my mom duties. I would have been quite cranky as I kept pushing forward and taken it out on the ones I love most. I would have taken it out on them in the name of "staying strong". That never did any of us any good!

Your child looks to you for guidance on how to act and feel. As such they are your biggest mirrors. They show you who you are by acting as you do. Sometimes the reflection is beautiful and sometimes you want to smash the mirror into pieces, so you don't have to face the truth of who you are. Your kid won't become who you tell them to be, they will become who you are, so do your best to be the adult you want them to become.

One of the greatest gifts you can give your child is to be imperfectly you. Allow them to see that you are human, you make mistakes, AND you have emotions too. No matter how hard you try to hide it when you are upset, your kids can still feel it. They are so aware of your body language and the shift in your energy. Many parents believe they are protecting their children when they tell the little white lie, "I'm fine." In truth, this lie can cause psychological damage to the child. It tells them their instinct was wrong and they can't trust what they swear they know. They can see the sadness in your face. They can feel the frustration built up inside you. So, they ask what is bothering you because they care, and they are met with this lie. Your words are not matching your way of being in the moment, and that confuses the hell out of your child. They stop trusting themselves.

Be honest! Tell them you are not okay in the moment. Let them see that all emotions are normal. It's okay to be sad, angry, disappointed, frustrated, tired, etc. If it's appropriate explain to them why you are feeling the way you are. If it's not an appropriate topic for them, still explain how you feel and that it's an adult issue. Thank them for asking and caring. Expressing your emotions in a healthy way allows them to do the same. Acknowledging and talking about how you feel will diffuse the emotions. Whereas, holding them in gives the emotion/s permission to explode like a bomb at some point in the future. Feel them now!

The second part of teaching your kid that all emotions are okay, is to also teach them that not all reactions are okay. It is okay to be angry at your sister. It is not okay to hit her! It is okay to feel frustrated that you can't solve the puzzle. It is not okay to throw the puzzle across the room!

Reactivity is something their dad and I have both struggled with our whole lives. So naturally it is something our kids have seen and emulated. They've seen our tempers flare, heard us scream, witnessed us slamming doors, and throwing things. So, we have no right to get mad at them for starting to react to their stress and emotions in the same way. It's our job to break this unhealthy pattern. To teach ourselves new ways to respond to our emotions, and then model that for our children.

One thing you can do is sit down as a family and make a list of appropriate ways you can choose to handle big negative emotions like anger or overwhelm. The techniques can be relaxing, silly, artistic, or physically active. Everyone in the family will have different calming methods that work for them. I like to take a walk to help work through my emotions. Sammy likes to read when she is upset. Sydney draws mad faces until she moves through it and can draw a happy face. Help your kids find what works for them and gently remind them to use these tools.

Want a copy of the list that hangs in our kitchen of ways my family chooses to calm down? Download your FREE PDF at www.katmullin.com.

What are some calming methods that work for you and your family? Let me know so we can try them and add them to our list!

Section Three

SAY NO TO LABELS

Speak to your children as if they are the wisest, kindest, most beautiful and magical humans on Earth, for what they believe is what they will become.

~Brooke Hampton~

How Labels Can Damage Your Child

My Sydney was labeled as shy once she started preschool. We honestly hadn't noticed that it was uncomfortable for her to talk to people before then. Her older sister is so outgoing, and they were always together. So, in my mind Sydney was as extroverted as Samantha. Yet when she was in a strange environment for the first time without Samantha to be her buffer, she got very quiet. She would not initiate playing with another child. She must be "shy". Once labeled we started to notice that she would hide behind me when an adult wanted to greet her. Reinforcing the notion that she's "just shy". It became a part of her personality. Her identity for a long time. Just as much so as the fact that she has brown eyes. Samantha started talking to people for her. If someone asked their names Samantha automatically responded with "I'm Sammy and she's Sydney". It took a few years for me to realize we were reinforcing the shy behavior. I stopped saying she was shy. I started asking her if she would like to say hi to someone. Sometimes she wouldn't, but sometimes she would. I gave her the opportunity and respected her wishes. At a restaurant I gave her the choice to place her own order. If she didn't want to, I did for her with a smile. If she wanted to, I told her she did a great job. Eventually Sydney told Samantha that she would like to start telling people her name herself. Now she starts conversations with strangers!

She's not shy after all! Imagine if she was never given the chance to be anything more than what we expected of her. Imagine all the opportunities she may have missed out on. The friendships she may not have made. The confidence she may never have developed.

Adults tend to forget that children are continually learning, growing, and becoming. They decide who a child is based off their behavior in a single situation and slap a forever label on said child. An article on Extension.unr.edu* describes three dangers of labeling your child.

1. Children believe what you say about them. They take it on as their identity and "live up" to the expectations placed on them.

2. This causes them to get stuck in the box you put them in. It literally stunts their personal growth and limits their potential.

3. Labeling a child also influences how others see them. Teachers, babysitters, and family members now have certain expectations of the child's behavior and may not go out of their way to see past the label to the child's true potential. If a teacher is told before the school year starts that Johnny behaves badly and gets bad grades, that is exactly what the teacher expects of him and will treat him accordingly. They may never push him to believe in himself and strive to be better.

Why do parents feel the need to label children? My best guess is that they get uncomfortable when their child acts a certain way in public. They feel it reflects on them, so they are quick to make excuses for it. "Oh, she's just shy. He is always nervous when trying something new. She's not great at math." This is where it is important that as a parent you shut off your own ego and choose not to care what society thinks of your child. You don't have to justify their behavior to anyone else, ever. Focus on your child in the moment and see what they need from you. And do your best to never let your child hear you label them when speaking to others. It does as much damage as saying it to their face. Let them grow and explore the world without the labels that can hold them back.

Connection #8

Label the Behavior

J ust like Sydney was not destined to be forever shy, your child is not their behavior. The best way to avoid limiting your child's potential is to label the behavior they are displaying instead of labeling them. They may act shy, angry, annoying, bossy, etc. in the moment. They are not a shy, angry, annoying, bossy, etc. person. They are not bad because they acted badly, and it is important they know this. The more you can acknowledge that your child is not their actions, the easier it becomes to see their positive attributes. This builds a deeper connection between the two of you. Let them know that regardless of behavior in the moment, you love them.

I know someone who was told repeatedly that they were angry as a child. In fact, his mom jokes he was angry in the womb. Did he act out in anger frequently? Yes. He also has a huge heart and cares deeply about others. He wants to be helpful and serve people. As an adult he wants to be the best husband and father possible. Yet he continually struggles with his pattern of reacting in anger. Imagine if his loving qualities were emphasized more than his angry traits when he was a child. If he was told it was okay to be angry and showed how to feel that anger in a healthier way. If instead of being told he was angry in the womb, he was told he was athletic, dancing, or full of excitement. Did his mom and the other adults in his life mean to instill this label as part of his identity? Absolutely not! His mom is an incredible woman who did her best to raise her kids as a working single mom. She gave them all she could and more. It is now his responsibility to heal these patterns and become the man he is meant to be.

When your child does something that you don't approve of tell them what they did was not okay without making them feel like they are not okay. Instead of "You are bad for hitting your sister." Try "I see you are angry, and it is okay to feel that way. It is not okay to hit people though." If your child sticks their tongue out or rolls their eyes at you, try "That is not kind." Instead of "You are rude!". You can refer to your list of calming techniques and help them choose one to use if they are open to it in the moment.

Another way of labeling children is by telling them what they are doing is making you upset. Maybe you had a tough day, so your patience is just not there when you get home. Your child may be acting in a way that normally does not bother you, but it is now. Instead of saying, "Stop that! You're annoying me!", try taking responsibility for your own feelings. You can tell your child, "I've had a long day and am feeling annoyed right now. I could use some space. Can you do that somewhere else?" This way the child does not feel it is their fault or that they are an annoying person. It's not a child's responsibility to know when a certain behavior is acceptable and when it will annoy you.

Let your child know that making mistakes is normal and says nothing about who they are as a person. Somewhere along the line my kids developed a habit of saying "I am so stupid" when they made a mistake. I remind them that we are all human and we all make mistakes. Even mom! And that those mistakes say nothing about our intelligence or our way of being. To be honest, I noticed that I had contributed to this feeling of being less than intelligent with my body language when they made mistakes. While my words were what they needed to hear after they expressed their belief about themselves, my initial response was not always okay. For example, if they spilt something I now needed to stop and clean up, I had a pattern of letting out a huge sigh and my body language would say "Ugh, come on!" and they felt that! Still working on that one. And the progress I recently noticed is more often than not I hear, "I FEEL stupid." That is a huge step up from "I AM stupid"! And we will continue to work on it until they know a mistake does not say anything negative about them.

Another tool you can implement is to avoid using universals like always, every time, never, everybody, nobody, etc. Do you know anyone who is ALWAYS anything? When I felt unheard, I would get upset and say, "Nobody listens to me!". Is that true? Of course not! And your child is not ALWAYS negative, positive, happy, upset, kind, rude, etc. Start to catch yourself when you are making a blanketed statement and reword it. For me, I now work on saying, "I feel unheard right now".

If you only take one thing away from this book, I hope it is this... You are your child's safe place. Home is the place they should feel comfortable letting their emotions out.

> You are your child's safe place.

When they are in meltdown mode, remember they are having a hard time, not giving you a hard time. Don't take it personally as it has nothing to do with you. Instead see if you can uncover what hidden emotion is underneath the tears and chaos so you can be empathetic to them. Another great piece of parenting advice I got when Samantha was a toddler was this… If your child behaves well in public, you are doing a great job! And I have held tight to this one. When they are melting down at home, I remind myself of all the compliments I get from others about how polite, kind, and helpful they are. This doesn't mean they are always perfect in public. They aren't ALWAYS anything.

This is why children can be an emotional mess when they get home from school. They had to hold all those big emotions in all day until they reached their safe place! My girls had a sleepover recently and I got a text from the mom that read, "I have literally never met more polite children in my whole entire life than your kids." Wow… what a compliment! My eyes got teary, and my heart swelled with pride. Guess what happened when they got home that night… Yup… HUGE meltdowns. I wanted to have my own damn meltdown in response! To remain calm, I kept reminding myself they held it all in for an entire day and I am their SAFE place to let it out. Plus, sleepovers usually mean little sleep, more junk food, and more screen time than normal and those all contribute to meltdowns! I say they are "detoxing" when this happens.

I've seen the negative effects that can happen when children are not allowed to express their emotions at home. When home is not a safe place to let it out, they may bottle it all up until they can't hold it in anymore. They may become super introverted, anxious, cause self-harm or start to bully others. I know kids who treat other kids badly when their parents aren't around and then act like angels at home to avoid getting in trouble. I'm not saying this is always the case. I am saying I would rather let my kids get it all out at home with me than to go into the world with bottled up emotions that need an outlet.

Do you have people close to you who say, "They never act like that when they're at my house!"? My response to that is, "Thank you, that means I am doing a good job. I am their safe place!". Be your kid's person. The one they can show all of themselves to without judgment. The one they know will not label them and will help them navigate it all.

Connection #9

Let Them Be Themselves

"Why can't you be more like your sister?"
Because I am not my sister!

"See Billy over there, he's not whining!"
Good for Billy for not being upset like I am!

These types of comparisons are damaging to a child's sense of self-worth. Every child is different and should never be compared to others. Your child is not like any other person in the world. Allow them to grow at their own pace without caring what other kids their age are doing. One of the most important things you can do for your child is to accept them for who they are as an individual. Even if it's a momentary wish that they were different, do your best to not express that to them. The moment might pass for you, but the comment you made could affect them negatively for a lifetime. They may spend their energy trying to please you instead of figuring out who they actually are.

Comparisons do not only harm the child you want to change. They can also do damage to the child you compare them to. Most people don't feel better about themselves when someone else is made to feel less than in comparison to them. It causes damage to the relationship between the two children that are being compared to each other. They may start to resent one another and treat each other unkindly. I know this happened between my siblings and I at times.

To help your child learn more about themselves, encourage them to explore new things. This is how they will find their own path. I know many people go into parenthood with dreams and expectations of who their child will grow up to be. It can be disappointing when they don't become who you envisioned them to be. Yet if you can embrace and love them for who they are, you will be able to let go of any disappointment you may have.

Matt had visions of his son following in his footsteps and playing baseball. He pictured them throwing the ball around together. Sawyer has an arm and would be great at it! We don't place those expectations on him though. We give all our kids options on what they want to do for activities and let them choose. And then we support them in it. So far, the girls have tried dance, soccer, and gymnastics. They both stuck with gymnastics. Sawyer has tried gymnastics, soccer (for one day), and most recently dance. And guess who was the proudest daddy at Sawyer's dance recital? Matt, of course! We also make sure our kids know they can change their minds and explore a new interest if they so desire. And Matt knows that even if none of them ever choose baseball or softball, he can certainly still throw a ball around with them. The kids love that time with him.

Gender labels are a surefire way to stunt a child's growth. It always makes my blood boil a bit when I hear things like, "Boys don't cry, girls can't play baseball, boys don't dance, girls shouldn't climb trees". I could go on and on as there are so many limiting misconceptions about gender roles. Let your boy know it's perfectly okay to cry so he doesn't grow up with all these bottled emotions that come out in anger and depression instead. Let your girl play baseball if she prefers it over softball. Let your boy dance and your girl climb trees. The outside world is going to give them enough grief over who they are. Be the person that helps them confidently do it anyway.

Another way to let your child be themselves is to allow them to explore nature. Let them get dirty (gasp)! Let them climb trees and rock

65

scramble. Let them dance in the rain and splash in puddles. Let them go barefoot. It's great for their immune system to play in the mud and dirt. And it will wash off. Have I mentioned what a clean freak I used to be? I definitely had to let go of that to allow my littles to just be kids. I am sure you've seen the "helicopter" parents at the playground. I wish they could see that they are passing their nervous traits down to their child and making them question their abilities. Climbing trees and play structures are a great way to build confidence. It's also great for their body awareness and hand-eye coordination. They must figure out how to get back down and be aware of where their body parts are as they do. Could they fall and get hurt? Yup! And they will learn to get back up. It's a great lesson for them!

Be your child's biggest cheerleader. Encourage them to explore what interests them. Don't compare them to others or limit what they are allowed to pursue. Accept them for their unique, amazing, spirited selves!

Connection #10

Even Positive Labels Can Be Harmful

I was pretty aware when I became a parent of the damage negative labels can do to kids. I was on people all the time about not calling my kids brats even jokingly. I let others know it wasn't okay to tell my child they were rude. Made sure people knew not to place gender roles on my kids. Anything that I felt shamed my child I spoke up about. Shame is a horrible feeling, and I never want anyone talking to my children in a way that makes them feel bad about themselves.

What I had not given much thought to is the damage positive labels can do. I mean, telling your kid they are good, kind, pretty, smart, etc. should make them feel great about themselves, right? It can. And it also can put them in a box and stunt their growth the same way negative labels can.

My Samantha is one of the kindest people I've ever met. She truly cares about others and wants to make people happy. It is a huge desire of hers to help those in need. When she was 7 years old, she wanted to help homeless people, so we set up a time with a local shelter for her to hand out blessing bags. Her heart is enormous, and I was constantly telling her so. "You are so kind" was something that came out of my mouth on an almost daily basis. Kindness became part of her identity and how she judged herself. Therefore, when she had moments of being unkind, as we all do, she felt shame and came down on herself harshly. How could she, "Samantha the Kind", treat someone badly? It was hard on her. It took me a while to see where it came from. My goal is to raise confident kids, and I was inadvertently contributing to her self-esteem in a negative way. I had to learn to reframe "You are kind" to "You did a kind thing". We talked a lot about how none of us are always one thing. We can all go against the nature of our true being and act differently. The key is to acknowledge when we aren't in alignment with ourselves without beating ourselves up for it.

> The key is to acknowledge when we aren't in alignment with ourselves without beating ourselves up for it.

Parents tend to label their kids to help themselves connect with their child's identity. "He's my athlete, this one's my smart one, She's my

68

funny one." These are all positive labels, but they still put your child in a box. Your child takes it on as who they are and may not try to be anything else. The athlete may want to try out for drama class but doesn't want to give up his athlete status. They may be afraid you would be disappointed if they did. The one who is not labeled the "smart one" may not try to get better grades because it is not expected of them, or they think they will never live up to the "smart one" so why try?

The best way to avoid stunting their potential with positive labels is the same as with negative labels... label the behavior instead. Tell your child what they said was funny instead of telling them they are funny, for example. Tell the athlete that they made a great catch. Tell the smart one they did great on their test, or you are impressed with how their brain figured out a problem. Do your best to avoid the labels, good or bad, that hold them back from their full potential.

Section Four

FREEDOM OF CHOICE

The greatest gifts you can give your children are the roots of responsibility and the wings of independence.

~Denis Waitley~

Their Voice Matters

I f one of your goals as a parent is to raise self-reliant, confident kids who trust themselves and trust you, encourage them to use their voice as often as possible. Another basic need every child has beyond food, shelter, and clothing is the need for control. You see this in toddlers who are just discovering they are a separate being from their parents. They are searching for their identity. This can look like the "terrible twos". When they start to throw fits over things that seem so little to you. Like how their sandwich is cut or which socks they wear that day. They just want a say in their life. Offering them choices and allowing them to pick can alleviate a lot of the meltdowns. Simply remembering to ask questions like, "How would you like your sandwich cut today? Triangles or squares?", "Would you like to wear the green or blue socks today?", or "Would you rather brush your teeth or put on your pajamas first?", gives them the autonomy they are looking for. Helps them feel like they have a voice, and it matters. And knowing they matter is everything as they grow into young adults getting ready to face the world.

Some people believe I give my children too much power. I disagree. Giving your child a voice in their life helps them believe in themselves. They start to trust that they are capable of making good decisions. I firmly stand by my decision as a parent to listen to my children's opinions. That includes a say in family decisions. It builds their confidence to know they are heard. That they are part of this family, and they have a voice in how we choose to live. That said, they also know that as the parents their dad and I have the final say. Especially when it comes to the big decisions, like where to live for instance. We will sit down as a family and allow everyone to state their opinions and give their reasons for why they feel the way they do. We make pros and cons lists together. We make sure they know everything they say matters to us, and we take it all into account when making our final decision. And as the adults we can't choose what they wish we would every time. Especially with three kids with different opinions. We can't always please everyone. Yet, even if they are disappointed with our decision, they know we did truly listen to them.

An important part of allowing them the freedom to choose is to hold them responsible for their decisions. Make sure they know they are the only one responsible for their words and actions. When they do something they shouldn't and their excuse is, "So and so told me to or did it first.", tell them "It doesn't matter what so and so said or did, you and only you are accountable for what you do". One of my favorite examples of this is when Sawyer was four. We were staying at a campground, and he knew the rule that none of the kids were allowed to go inside their friends' RVs unless we met the parents first and gave the ok. He didn't know I was watching him. A boy his age kept telling him to come inside his trailer. I could see Sawyer was debating if he should. He would start to walk over to the door and then stop. This went on for a bit with the other boy repeatedly telling him to come in. Finally, Sawyer couldn't take the peer pressure anymore and screamed, "I am responsible for my actions, and I am NOT coming in!" Oh, the pride I felt in that moment.

I feel the need to be clear on something here. When I say, "hold them responsible for their decisions", I do not mean by shaming them. I do not presume to tell you how to "discipline" your child. I will say that for us, shaming, blaming, yelling, forcing insincere apologies, time-outs, spankings, etc., have never worked. It has only made them feel bad about themselves, and no one can grow and learn when they don't feel good about themselves. It also caused damage to the trusting bond we had as parent/child. How can I help my child trust themselves if they don't trust me? What has worked for us? Talking to them with understanding, asking them their reasons for doing what they did, letting them know they made a mistake and that's okay, explaining to them why what they did was not okay or dangerous, coming up with ways to handle things better next time they are in a similar situation, talking about their feelings on what happened, having them write/draw about it, and if it's a sibling fight we may ask them to list 5-10 things they love about each other. These are the ways I have found that give them a voice and create a lasting positive change in their behavior and decision making.

For your child to grasp the concept of taking responsibility for themselves, you must be their example by taking ownership of your own actions. When your decisions lead to a win, let your child see you celebrate. If you mess up, own it! Apologize when appropriate. Yes, even apologize to your child if he/she is the one you slighted. I've had multiple family members scold me for apologizing to my child. Said I was giving away my power as the adult. I tell them I will always say sorry to my child if I do something wrong. How else will they learn to apologize when they mess up? Let your child see you fail and succeed and take responsibility for it all.

Connection #11

Empower Your Child with Choices

Critical thinking is a skill that you can help your child develop by allowing them to make decisions. A child who is constantly told what, when, and how to do things cannot become self-reliant. There is a meme I love that is a parent talking to a child and says, "Honey, when you grow up I want you to be assertive, independent, and strong-willed. But while you're a kid, I want you to be passive, pliable, and obedient." It just doesn't work that way! For them to stand up for themselves as adults you must allow them to stand up for themselves now. Start with the little things.

Let your child pick their own outfits. Nothing screams confidence like a young one running around in mismatched socks, striped leggings, a polka dot shirt, and a bowtie! Or rocking their Superman/girl costume at the grocery store. I personally love seeing the unique and wild styles they come up with. When my Sydney started preschool her favorite things to wear were pajamas and mismatched shoes and socks. I have a photo of her ready for school wearing two pajama tops, pajama shorts, one tall rainbow sock, a short sock, mismatched shoes, and a cowgirl hat. She couldn't have been more pleased with her choices that day! Samantha went through a phase of wearing jeans to bed. I couldn't imagine it was comfortable, but it made her happy. I also have photos of her midsummer loving life in a Christmas dress at the playground. Sawyer is currently sporting neckties clipped on to his basketball style tank top, rain boots even on sunny days, and one fingerless glove! He also loves leggings. A few family members have felt the need to question us letting him wear leggings as a boy. Luckily for Sawyer we don't allow others' opinions on what's acceptable influence how he dresses. He is all about the way something feels, and leggings are comfortable. It's his choice.

Hairstyle is another independent choice you can give your child. Do they like their hair long or short? Do they like fun colors? My mother used to cut my hair super short because she didn't like brushing it. My mother was not a hairdresser. When I say she cut it short, there was no cute style happening! I hated it. I was called a boy frequently and it didn't feel good. My self-esteem suffered

76

because of it. Sydney's hair is currently long, but she has had the cutest and most stylish short cuts! On the other hand, Sawyer rocks long hair with the best of them. By the time he was four it was halfway down his back. He was called a girl frequently, but it rarely bothered him. Again, family members felt the need to make comments about it. Threaten to cut his hair even. And he would tell them himself he loved his hair and didn't want to cut it. Not long after he turned four, he decided he wanted to chop it all off. I waited about a month to be sure he meant it and wouldn't regret it before I took him to the hairdresser. He loved his new fresh do because it was his choice to cut it. He continues to grow it long and then cut it again. It's always his choice.

Allow your child to choose their own activities and sports as well. I already covered this in the last section, but it's worth repeating. Don't expect your child will love the same things you love to do. I'm sure you've seen the parent who tries to relive their youth through their kids. Insist their kid does the same sport they did. Criticize their child if they aren't the best at it. Don't be that parent! It's not fair to the child. Matt loves baseball. Sawyer likes it but not enough to choose it as his activity. If he ever does decide to try baseball it will be his decision. Let them choose from a list of activities and hobbies that are within your budget. Even if they aren't the best at it. If it lights them up, cheer them on!

Part of encouraging your child's independence is letting them make mistakes. It can be so much easier to just do everything for them. It saves time, things get done the "right" way, and you keep your sanity. In the long run though, it is harmful to their confidence and self-esteem. It decreases their ability to be able to take care of themselves as they get older. The old adage, "Give a man a fish and you feed him for a day. Teach a man to fish and you feed him for a lifetime.", is so true. I used to have the hardest time letting my kids help in the kitchen because the mess would give me anxiety. I had to learn to put myself in the mindset of letting go. Messes can be cleaned up. How else will they learn to cook for themselves if I don't let them help me? As the youngest of seven children, I didn't have to do much around the house. My only real chore was washing dishes. When I moved out on my own, I had no clue how to cook a real meal, scrub a bathtub clean, or manage my finances. I was forever the "baby" in my family, and that did not serve me.

Give your child responsibilities, and then let them do it as best they can and praise them for it. For some it comes more naturally to criticize than praise. Make it a priority to compliment even when things aren't perfect. I had to learn this the hard way when my girls started cleaning the house. I would point out where they missed a spot dusting or criticize the streaks on the mirror. I then saw the look on their faces that said, "I suck." Matt actually told me I should leave the house while they clean so I'm not tempted to "help" them. Ouch! Lesson learned.

There is no need to hover over your child or "correct" how they are doing something. That teaches them nothing. In fact, they are more likely to "mess up" if you are watching them like a hawk. It makes them nervous. Let them do things their way and see if it works or not. If it doesn't, they will try something else until they figure it out. Help only if they ask for it. If they get discouraged and say they can't do something, remind them that they are capable and it's okay to not get things right the first time. Ask them what they could try next time. Experimenting is how they figure things out.

This way of parenting requires two things of you...

One: Don't give a blankety blank what society, family, friends or anyone else say. Do what's best for you and your family. If it makes your child happy to wear mismatch clothes in public, let them! No one else's opinion should matter. If it does matter to you what others think, ask yourself why? How is it a problem for you if others judge what your child wears? Parents sometimes hide behind, "I am protecting them from being made fun of." While none of us want to see our child get their feelings hurt, we can't protect them from everything. Someone will always find a reason to put others down. Your child will deal with hurt feelings no matter how hard you try to avoid it. Not allowing them to express themselves through their clothes and activities will only send them the message that you do not believe they are not good enough as they are. That will do more damage in the long run than a mean comment at the playground. When someone does belittle your child, they will decide for themselves if it is worth changing their style to avoid the rudeness.

1. Do what's best for you and your family.

Two: You will have to let go of control and allow them

2. Let go of control and allow them to find their own way.

to find their own way. Remember, they are their own person and it's not about you. Controlling what your child does, says, how they act, who they want to be, etc., once again sends the message that they are not worthy as they are. Where can you let go of control as a parent? Pay attention to where you may be overly controlling your child. Is it necessary? Could you step back and give them a say over the situation? Could you encourage them to choose for themselves? Would it be appropriate to give them the power?

A recent lesson on letting go that I had myself was with Sydney. I am a minimalist, and she is not! She likes to collect random things like bottle caps and receipts. Not receipts from special occasions mind you. She doesn't care if it's a grocery store receipt, from the gas station, or whatever. It gives me anxiety when I see the crumpled-up receipts mixed in with her toys in her cabinet. I helped her clean out the cabinet the other day, and I wanted so badly to just throw them all out! I had to remind myself that she is her own person and has a right to her collection even if I don't understand it. Maybe someday I will see why she has this attachment. Maybe I won't. Either way, for now I just need to respect it. So, I took some deep breaths and helped her fold them neatly and place them in a zipped change purse. She was grateful I accepted her and her random collection as is.

The more control you can give your child over their own life, the less likely they will be to seek power in negative ways. This means less tantrums, less rebellion, less indecisiveness, and less depression. Instead, there will be more confidence, more self-esteem, more cooperation, and more independence.

Connection #12

Boundaries are Self-Care

Teaching your child how to set boundaries from a young age is crucial to their wellbeing as an adult. Many adults today grew up not being allowed to have personal boundaries. We were the child and therefore did what we were told. In fact, saying no to an adult could have gotten a child smacked in some households! I personally had no idea what boundaries were and why I should set them. The word "NO" was almost impossible for me to say. It would feel like it was physically lodged in my throat. I became a people pleaser, and I resented the people I was "pleasing" because of it. Was it their fault? In most cases, no. I allowed them to take advantage because I didn't know any better. I am a giver and a helper by nature. Yet eventually I would feel hurt if someone wasn't reciprocating. I missed out on doing so much I wanted to do because I wouldn't speak up and give my opinion. I would just go with what the other person suggested. In romantic relationships

I held the belief that if someone cared about me, they would automatically respect me. NOT TRUE! I was in my mid-forties before I learned why boundaries are important and how to set them. I had to learn to love and respect myself first if I wanted others to treat me well. My biggest lesson during this time in my life...

"Strong relationships have strong boundaries!"

~Kat Mullin~

So how can you teach your child to set boundaries for themselves? An article on AllProDad.com* talks about teaching your kid to have Clarity, be Clear, and be Consistent. I will add to that, give them their voice. Allow them to make choices and give their opinion. In fact, ask them their opinion on things often. Allow them to have and talk about their feelings and emotions so they don't get bottled up. And teach them that "No" is a good word! It's only two little letters, but it really is the hardest word to say if you are taught it is bad to do so. Don't just tell them it's okay to say no. Allow them to say no to you!

Even though I hadn't learned boundaries for myself yet, when I had kids, I knew I wanted them to be able to say no. I wouldn't allow others, not even family, to force affection on them. Samantha went through a stage when she was 2 years old where she did not enjoy hugs. Yet adults often felt like they had the right to require a hug from her. "But I came to visit you, don't I get a hug for that?" Hell no you don't! My child said she doesn't want one. She is physically pulling away from you. And the look of discomfort on her face is palpable! Back off!!! Of course, I said it nicer than that because I was still a people pleaser myself. "She would not like a hug right now." Or "Sammy, would you like a hug? It's okay if you don't right now." That way they could hear her say no. I developed the habit of asking for hugs and kisses first myself, and if my child said no, I respected that. It's their body and they have a right to not be touched. I talk with my kids about body bubbles and how everyone has one. I make sure they know they have a right to protect theirs, and that it is important they respect others' body bubbles also.

I did not have that right when I was younger. If we were at a family party, I was expected to be "respectful" and hug all the adults hello and goodbye. It did not matter if I didn't want to. It did not matter if I was uncomfortable around certain adults. I didn't have a say in it. And that is one of the reasons I didn't feel I could say no as a teenager when boys started wanting more than hugs. Think about that! Let your child say no now so they can later. They will thank you for it.

Teaching boundaries goes way beyond sex or physical affection. It is about showing your child the importance of creating a safe environment for themselves. It is about teaching them their worth so they know when someone is treating them less than. At my kids' ages now, it is all about

> It is about teaching them their worth so they know when someone is treating them less than.

friendships. We are having regular discussions about what true friendship looks like. How do you want the people you allow in your life to treat you? How do you want them to treat themselves and others? Do you feel good when you are around this person? What values do you want them to have? What is important to you in a friendship? Is it okay for someone to be "kind" to you one day but treat you badly the next day? What does bullying look like and how can you stand up to it? Are you treating your friends the way you want to be treated? Do you display the same values you expect others to have? We have all these talks regularly.

Samantha has even written down what she values in a person and what qualities they need to have to be in her life. And now she is learning how to navigate when someone doesn't have those qualities. Does she still hang out with them? How many chances does she give them? Which qualities are essential, and which are nice but not necessary? What if it is a group activity and she wants to be with the other kids that are there? These questions do not always have easy answers, but only she can answer them for herself. Wish someone taught me to do that when I was younger!

People have suggested to me that my children need to have thicker skin and toughen up to survive in this world. I was brought up this way. Walked around like I was tough, and nothing bothered me. It's a defense mechanism that doesn't work. People who pretend they aren't hurting still hurt. They just bury it down deep. They may grow up to numb the pain with addictions. The pain may come through the body in the form of a disease. And the worst part of teaching our kids to toughen up is that it gives the bullies permission to keep hurting others!! I certainly don't want to raise my kids to allow abuse in their lives. I want to raise them to set boundaries and stick to them. To know their value and worth, and not allow others to mistreat them just so they "belong".

"It's not our job to toughen our children up
to face a cruel and heartless world.
It's our job to raise children who will
make the world a little less cruel and heartless."

~L. R. Knost~

Teaching and allowing your child to set boundaries will help them know their self-worth. They will be more likely to build friendships based in trust, mutual respect, and kindness. To pick a partner who values them. To stand up to the boss that tries to take advantage of them. To know who has their back when it counts. To know when to walk away. That is a true gift to your future adult child.

Connection #13

Goal Setting

In the last few months, the kids and I started setting daily goals together. I've talked with them in the past about having big goals in life, and how having something to strive for gives you purpose. We talk about the sense of pride they will have in themselves when they accomplish their goals. As discussed in an article on LinkedIn.com*, there are multiple benefits to teaching your child to set and achieve goals. One of them being, "Grow a sense of purpose". This improves self-image and builds confidence.

Goal setting, like boundaries, are relatively new for me. I was the type who knew certain things in life I wanted to achieve, but never sat down to figure out how I was going to get there. Some I still achieved because I was either motivated enough or there was a clear path. Most goals fell to the wayside because they were too overwhelming, and I had no clue where to start. A few years ago, I hired a life coach to help me gain clarity on my personal and professional lives. She taught me how to see the big picture and work backwards from there. Little steps to the big goal. We set 6 goals for me to achieve in 6 months. We broke them down into what I would need to do monthly, weekly, and daily to reach them. I created a vision board to look at every morning and night to help me envision the reality I wanted. Once a week we discussed my progress. What were my wins that week? What did I not accomplish and why? It worked. I rocked those 6 goals!

I am not going that in-depth with the kids just yet. However, teaching them to set and accomplish even the tiniest goals now will help them reach their bigger life goals. My three kids are different ages with different dreams. Samantha and Sydney may set goals of stretching daily because it helps with their gymnastics. Side note: Samantha just achieved one of her biggest goals in life to date. When she was 5 years old, she set her goal of making the competitive team for gymnastics. This is huge for her! Sawyer, on the other hand, may set a goal of "eat candy". Okay! I let him have a piece of candy so he can feel accomplished checking off that goal! Of course, if it's something that could be harmful to them, like jumping off a tall bridge with no bungee, I wouldn't allow it just so they can check the box. Safety trumps being able to say you did it.

This is how we go about daily goal setting...

Every night we look at our list from that day and check off what we accomplished. If we each check them all off, that's awesome. If any of us do not check them all off, that is okay! When we first started doing this routine Sydney felt compelled to get everything she wrote down checked off. We had a good talk about how important it is to look at what you did accomplish. Not what you didn't. She was further than she would have been if she didn't strive for any goals that day and that's worth celebrating. She learned to write down as many goals as she wanted without pressuring herself to complete every single one. To prioritize which were the most important that day. This is important to note because goal setting can either increase or decrease self-esteem. If done right, it gives purpose and does wonders for confidence. That is the goal with goal setting!

After we check off our wins, we say what we are most grateful for, proud of, or enjoyed most that day. We also talk about any disappointments if anyone wants to. Then we write down our goals for the next day. All of this has an added benefit of giving some structure and routine to our days. I am not a very regimented person, so this is one way we get a balance of freedom and routine in our lives.

I have done vision boards with my girls in the past too. It mostly consisted of American Girl dolls and accessories they wanted, but it did also have higher goals of gymnastics and surfing, as well as the type of person they wanted to be. This could be a very fun activity for you to do with your child also.

When we first started doing the daily goal setting, I figured I would be "nice" and give them weekends off. Sydney was having none of that. She loved the way it made her feel to check off the goals she set. This really is a great way to build self-esteem, confidence, as well as a sense of pride and accomplishment. And when you allow them to choose their own goals, you give them the freedom of choice.

Connection #14

Let Intuition Guide Them

Teach your child to trust their intuition, gut feeling, divine guidance, instinct, inner knowing, higher-self, or whatever you want to call it. The unconscious mind knows, and if you can listen to it, you will not be steered wrong. Neither will your child. This is one thing I really wish someone taught me when I was young!

What is the unconscious mind? It runs your body. It is why you don't have to think about breathing or making your heart pump. The unconscious mind keeps a blueprint of your perfect health. It also stores ALL your memories and filters new experiences based off those memories. Your unconscious mind is why you have patterns of reactivity or certain behaviors. It is where your beliefs are stored and where your emotions come from. Your emotions are how your unconscious mind communicates with you. It also "talks" to you through your body via dis-ease.

I will never forget the first time I "listened" to my unconscious mind. I didn't know that is what I was doing. I said I was following my gut. It told me to give up my seat in dental hygiene school and take off in my car! What??? Give up a good career and just drive aimlessly?! The feeling was so strong that I couldn't ignore it. So, I called the school and told them I would not be starting in the fall. I fit what I could in the back of my SUV and drove. I decided to head towards California from Cape Cod, MA where I grew up. I was going to go alone with no plan, but I got lucky, and my cousin asked if he could join me. We made a very flexible plan heading towards CA. Because of him, I saw way more of this country than I would have on my own, and I am grateful for his company. I had no home to go to, knew not one soul in CA, and had no job. I didn't want to have to get there. I wanted to take my time and be able to settle anywhere along the way if I fell in love with a certain area. My cousin was coming for the ride, but then heading back to MA. Wherever I ended up he was not staying. I made it to San Diego and fell in love. It was the first time I felt like I was home. Listening to that "crazy" feeling telling me to give up everything was the BEST thing I ever did for myself. I want my kids to always let their intuition guide them so they can live their best lives with no doubts or regrets.

So how do you listen to your unconscious mind? You can meditate, journal, and/or simply ask it questions and wait for the answer. If you

> I want my kids to always let their intuition guide them so they can live their best lives with no doubts or regrets.

can ask out loud that is better, but it still works to ask silently. Be sure to direct your question to your unconscious mind. "Unconscious mind...", followed by your question. The first thing that pops into your mind is your answer. Don't think about it! Just go with the first answer you get.

A simple example of this was a time Sawyer was picking out a candy at the convenience store. He became very overwhelmed with all the choices! I asked him to stop and relax for a second. Then told him to ask his unconscious mind which candy he wants. I directed him to hold a candy in his hand and ask if he wanted it. The look on his face when he got the answer was priceless. "It said no!". Ok, try another. He did this a few times until he got a yes, and he was so happy with his choice.

The answer may not always be immediate. Samantha came to me one time and said she felt sad but didn't know why. I told her it was okay to not know why as long as she allowed the feeling. However, if she really wanted to know the reason, she could ask her unconscious mind. She did but did not get an answer right away. I let her know that was all right and told her to go about her bedtime routine. It may come to her later. Sure enough, about five minutes later, she let me know she got the answer. We had just settled down in a new neighborhood after traveling for a few years in our RV. She was happy to make a steady friend for the first time since traveling. She made amazing friends during our travels, but we always moved on and they would have to say goodbye (for now). She finally had this friend who lived just down the street and the friend was leaving for a couple of months. She wasn't even consciously aware that her friend leaving was influencing her mood until she asked why she was sad.

Growing up and for most of my adult life I had the limiting belief of "I don't know". Sydney now struggles with it. When I ask her questions, she immediately gets frustrated and says she doesn't know. Unlike her siblings, it is not easy for her to simply ask and get an answer. It is like she blocks herself from receiving. We are working on this all the time. When she says she doesn't know I remind her she does know. The unconscious mind always knows. There are many ways you can "hear" your inner guidance. An amazing book that teaches these ways is *The Emotion Code**. The author speaks about using muscle testing to discover your trapped emotions and release them. It is fascinating. I taught Sydney his method called "The Sway Test". To use this method, you stand still and say a truth or ask a yes or no question you know the answer to. For example, I could say "I love my dog" and notice if my body sways forward or backwards. That is now my "yes" answer. Then I say a false statement like, "I hate my dog" and test that the "no" answer sways in the opposite direction. Once the yes and no directions are established you can ask yes or no questions and receive the answer from your unconscious mind. Test the yes and no directions each time you use this method as they may change. This works better for Sydney than directly asking and listening for her answers.

Communicating with the unconscious mind is another way your child can have freedom in making his/her own choices. It builds their trust in themselves to be able to access the answers. They can go forth confidently knowing they are making the best decisions for themselves. The younger they can start connecting with their unconscious the better chance they have at growing up to live their authentic life and be a Badass Human!

One Last Message to YOU!

"Love Yourself to Love Your Family."

~Kat Mullin~

The best thing I did for myself and my family when I first started my self-awareness journey was to become a morning person. This was not easy as someone who comes from a long line of night owls! As parents we all need time to ourselves to fill our own cups. I started getting up before the kids to meditate, do yoga, write, and walk the dogs. That way when they woke up, I was in the right mindset to greet them. When I waited to get out of bed until they woke me up, I struggled with being kind. It was hard to be woken to the needs of others! I am not saying you must be a morning person too. I am saying it is important to find time to put yourself first!

Affirmations, when done right, can be a great way to start your day. I created a list of Positive Affirmations for Parents to remind us we are worthy of this job! Download your FREE PDF here: www.katmullin.com

Your self-awareness journey has a ripple effect that extends to your loved ones and beyond. If you want to raise your children to be confident individuals who take responsibility for themselves, you must start with the most important person in your life, YOU! It is time to unlearn the patterns that no longer serve you. It is time to be your child's best example of how an authentic life full of joy and passion is lived. It is time to discover the true you.

To make an effective, immediate, and long-lasting change in yourself it must be done at the unconscious level where all those patterns and beliefs are stored. My unique Breakthrough Coaching does just that so you can be free to live your life in the present moment. Not from a place of the past. You will release stuck negative emotions and let go of the limiting beliefs that prevent you from living your best life. You will believe in yourself and be able to teach your child to do the same!

I wrote this book for you. To guide you on how to be present with your child as you start healing your own inner child. Congratulations... You've already taken the first step in your journey by reading this book. Be proud! Now it's time to take the next step. To choose you...

100

www.katmullin.com

Book your FREE thirty-minute Discovery Call at
www.calendly.com/katmullin

"The most important work you will ever do will
be within the walls of your own home."

~Unknown~

Acknowledgments

Through the years, many have had a huge impact on my life by supporting, inspiring, and mentoring me in different ways. I am truly blessed to have such amazing people in my life to look up to. It is impossible to thank everyone, and I apologize for anyone not listed. Please know that I appreciate you greatly.

First and foremost a huge thank you to my Badass Humans! Samantha, Sydney, and Sawyer... I LOVE YOU! This book would not have happened without you three. Thank you from the bottom of my heart for allowing me to share your stories. I truly hope they help many other families. And to your sister, Taylor Hope, in the Spiritual World for showing me I am meant to be of service in this world. I love you always Taylor!

To Matthew, THANK YOU for not giving up when we weren't sure we could become parents. It is because of your dedication to becoming a father that we have these amazing souls with us today. You are LOVED!

To my mom and dad, Sylvia and Jack, for doing YOUR best. I always knew I was loved. I miss you both every day and love you forever. And to my six older siblings who helped teach me about life as the baby of the family…. Thank you. I love you guys bunches!

To my MIL, Rita, for taking me in as if I was your own from day one. You have had our backs and given us more support than anyone could ever ask for. I love you and appreciate you!

To the Middendorf and Taylor clans…. I love you all!!! There's way too many of you to mention individually, but know I cherish every single one of you.

To my amazing friends… you know who you are! I am beyond blessed to have friends that are family. That support me, believe in me, encourage me, call me out when I need it, and love me no matter what. Growing up I always wanted those forever friends. I am one lucky girl to have found them!!

To my NLP peeps at Recalibrate 360… you guys rock! Thank you for helping me get over my self-doubt so I could finally believe in ME!

And now for the people that have inspired and mentored me without even knowing it! People I turn to when I need to be reminded that we are all capable of greatness…

Dean Graziosi and Tony Robbins, you have created such an amazing community full of support. You inspire me every time I hear your voices! Derek Rydall, for The Abundance Project podcast. It got me through some hard times. Rhonda Byrne whose book *The Secret* changed my life, and to all the amazing souls that collaborated with her to bring the concept of Manifestation to the world. Gary Vee who proves you can f*ing inspire people with my favorite word! Glennon Doyle for her candid writings about her own family's truths. Brené Brown for proving that vulnerability is strength. Hands Free Mama, Rachel Macy Stafford, for reminding me what it means to choose love and be present with my own family. The Badass Manifester, Ashley Gordon, whose podcast lifted me up when I was down. Vince Gowmon for being an activist for children. He reminds us that what kids need most is more love and more time. Dayna Martin for showing the world it is a beautiful thing to trust your kids and allow them to express themselves.

To the people who helped me get this book DONE! To the Life on Fire community for putting together the course, Bestseller on Fire, that pushed me over the edge to finally follow my dream of becoming an author. Dave Pomeroy (aka The Tech Guy) for putting up with my multitude of changes and directions over the last couple of years and staying by my side (other side of the computer that is!) through it all. You see my vision! To my friends who so generously gave this a pre-read and offered feedback on how to make it better. And to Starr Loutsis with Aligning Purpose Publishing for literally getting this book into the world!

And of course to The Universe for the eternal guidance and wisdom. For Light, Love and Connection to ALL.

I am forever grateful to you ALL and have so MUCH LOVE for everyone of you!!!

About Kat

Kat Mullin is your Self-Awareness Coach and Communication Expert. She has over twenty years of experience in the personal development industry. Her *passion* to serve others has led her to become a Holistic Health Practitioner, Certified Massage Therapist, Reiki Master Practitioner, Master NLP Breakthrough Coach, Master Practitioner of Time Line Therapy, Master Practitioner of Hypnosis, and Published Author.

Kat's hobbies and interests include hiking, traveling, walking in nature, reading, writing, and adventuring with her family and dogs.

Her greatest teachers are her children. She is Mom to 3 amazing souls with whom she continues to learn and grow. It is through being a mom that Kat started to learn about generational patterns and the limiting beliefs that can be inherited from our ancestors. It has become her *purpose* in life to help as many people as possible break the patterns that no longer serve them and start their greatest journey of all... learning to fully love and accept themselves. When someone truly loves themself, they make more meaningful connections with their family and loved ones. Her vision with this goal is to free future generations from carrying on the negative cycles so they have a fresh start at living their own authentic lives.

Kat's unique methods guide you and your family to achieve effective communication with each other, release stuck negative emotions, and free yourselves from the limiting beliefs that hold you back from living your best lives.

Website:
www.katmullin.com

Email:
kat@katmullin.com

Special <u>FREE</u> Bonus Gift for You
To become more self-aware and align with your truth go to <u>www.freegiftfromkat.com</u> **for your FREE BONUS RESOURCES**

Resources

The benefits of spending quality one on one time with your child

By Genevieve Simperingham

Peaceful Parent Institute, www.peacefulparent.com

How to Create One-on-one Time With Each of Your Kids

By Amy Morin, LCSW

July 26, 2021

www.VeryWellFamily.com

The Whole-Brain Child

By Daniel J. Seigel, M.D. and Tina Payne Bryson, Ph.D.

Published by Bantam Books Trade Paperbacks

New York, copyright 2011

The Key To Your Child's Heart (7 Ways It Works)

By Janet Lansbury, November 14, 2011

www.Janetlansbury.com, elevating child care

Avoid labeling your child

By YaeBin Kim and Heidi Petermeier, 2019

University of Nevada, Reno www.Extension.unr.edu

5 Tips for Teaching Your Kids about Boundaries

All Pro Dad, Mark Merrill www.allprodad.com

5 Benefits of Goal Setting for Children

By Amali Prescilla, November 25, 2020

www.linkedin.com

The Emotion Code

By Dr. Bradley Nelson   Foreword by Tony Robbins

Published by St. Martin's Essentials

New York, copyright 2019

Made in the USA
Columbia, SC
10 December 2022

72382401R00070